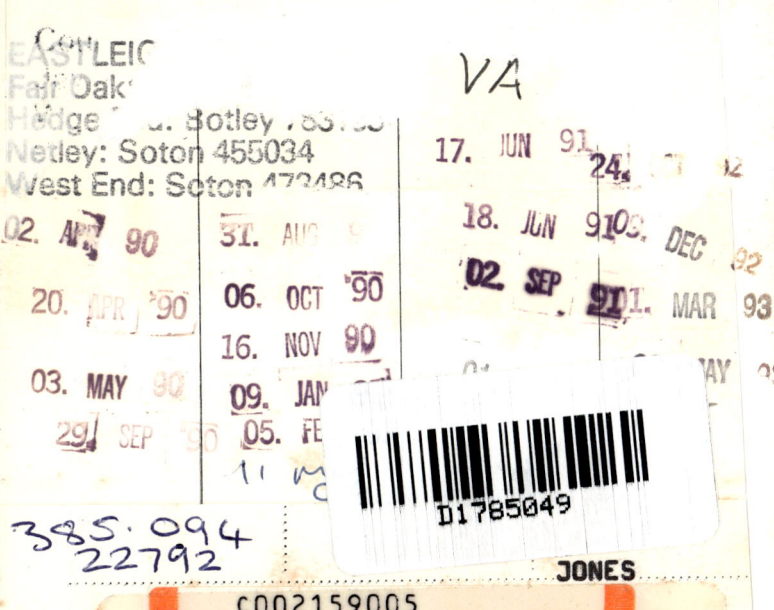

Copyright 1988 Peter Jones

First Published by Picton Publishing (Chippenham) Ltd. 1989

ISBN 0-948251-25-X

British Library Cataloguing in Publication Data

Jones, Peter

The Pompey Train

1. Hampshire.   Portsmouth.   Railway Services

1. Title

385.09422.792

Printed in Great Britain by Picton Print
Citadel Works, Bath Road, Chippenham, Wilts.

Part of the Southern Railway system

Portsmouth & Southsea Station frontage, circa 1910 (Photo Anon)

INTRODUCTION

The routes and structures of the early railways were determined by a variety of causes. Occasionally it was commonsense engineering that was the factor, but more often it could be a mixture of plain politics and financial infighting. But in the case of Portsmouth it was fear of invasion.

The naval base had been strongly defended for centuries. There are great stone structures built for Henry VIII and there are concrete blocks which were part of a defence against midget submarines. But some of the largest structures were created against a Napoleonic invasion. In the waters of Spithead the tiny island fortresses are prominent. To the north of the island of Portsmouth, Portsdown Hill also has substantial defences. The forts there were built so that the guns could face north. This was to counter the threat of a force landing on a soft underbelly of coast and marching round to sneak up unawares. Incidentally the fact of north facing defence gave rise to another of those innumerable stories where we are told 'they had the plans upside down you know ...'

The very first railway to serve the area didn't actually go to Portsmouth at all. It branched off the London to Southampton line at what is now Eastleigh, and went in a fairly straight line down to Gosport. This has left a legacy at Fareham where the minor line goes straight through the station whereas the main Southampton to Portsmouth line calls for a couple of very sharp curves.

But the good citizens of Portsmouth were not satisfied by a trip to London that called for a first leg which was a ferry journey going in the opposite direction. The story of the battles

1

PORTSMOUTH, FAREHAM, GOSPORT, NETLEY.

WEEK DAYS.

		a.m.	a.m.	a.m.	a.m.	a.m.	a.m.	a.m.	a.m.	a.m.	a.m.	a.m.	a.m.	a.m.	a.m.	a.m.	a.m.	a.m.	a.m.	a.m.	p.m.	a.m.	p.m.	p.m.	a.m.
RYDE (Pier Head)	dep.							7 40								8 50		10 10							10 45
PORTSMOUTH HARB'R	,,							7 40								9 30		10 45							noon.
PORTSMOUTH TOWN	,,	12 20		6 10	7 3			7 43	8 5	9 40		9 4				9 35	9 50	10 55							12 0
Fratton	,,	12 23		6 13	7 7			7 53	8 10	9 44		9 7				9 39	9 53	10 55							12 3
Cosham	,,			6 22	7 16			8 5	8 19			9 16				9 49	5 11	6							12 15
Porchester	,,	12 31		6 27	7 23			8 12				9 22				9 56	12 11	13							12 22
FAREHAM	arr.	12 40		6 34	7 28			8 18	8 29	9 0		9 28				10 2	10 18	11 19							12 29
Stokes Bay	dep.															9 30	10 50			11 85					
Gosport Road	,,															9 34	10 54			11 30					
Gosport	,,			7 15				8 0			8 45					9 40	10 5 11 0			11 5					
Fort Brockhurst	,,			7 19				8 4			8†45					9 44	5 11 4			11 2					
FAREHAM	arr.			7 25				8 11								9 51 10 15 11 11				12 16					
FAREHAM	dep.	12 41		6 37	7 33			8 24	8 31	9 1		9 29				10 5	10 27	11 36				12 20			12 31
Botley	,,	12 52		6 47				8 38								10 17	11 31					12 35			
EASTLEIGH	arr.	1 2		6 56				8 49								10 27	11 41					12 43			
Swanwick	dep.			7 41					8 39			9 37					10 29	11 41							12 40
Bursledon	,,			7 46					9 12			9 42					10 34	11 49							12 45
Netley	,,			7 53			8 17		8†49	18		9 48					10 42	11 56							12 52
Sholing	,,			7 57			8 22		8 53			9 53					10 47	12 1							
Woolston	,,			8 0			8 25		8 56			9 56					10 50	12 4							12 58
Bitterne	,,			8 5			8 30		9 1	9 27		10 1					10 55	12 9							1 3
St. Denys	,,			8 8			8 33		9 4			10 4					10 58	12 12							1 7
Northam	,,			8 13						9 33		10 9						12 14							
SOUTHAMPTON TN.	arr.			8 16					9 36			10 12						12 21							
(for Docks)	dep.			7 20										10 5								12 45			1 16
Southampton West	,,			Stp. 7 27	8 40			9 15						10 8	11 9							12 52			1 20
Millbrook	,,			7 31				9 19							11 14							12 56			1 25
Redbridge	,,			7 36	8 47			9 34						10 19	11 16							1 1			1 30
Nursling	,,			7 41	8 52										11 21							1 6			
N'THAMPTON TN.	dep.			8 45																		12 55			12 55
Northam	,,			6 48																		12 58			12 58
St. Denys	,,			6 52																		1 2			
Swaythling	,,			6 56																		1 5			
EASTLEIGH	arr.	1 30	7 6		7 55	8 59					9 26	10 40			12 10						1 13			
Chandlers Ford	,,		7 13		8 2	9 4					9 35	10 57			12 18						1 20			
Romsey	,,	1 45	7 24		†11†48	9 17	9 37				9 44	10 58	11 28			12 27					1 14	1 29		1 40
Mottisfont	dep.			7 57							9 57										1 22			
Horsebridge	,,			8 3							10 2										1 28			
Stockbridge	,,			7 35 8 11							10 8										1 35			
Fullerton Junction	,,			7†41 8 16							10 12										1 42			
Clatford	,,			8 24							10 16										1 48			
Andover Town	,,			8 29							10 23										1 53			
ANDOVER JUNCTION	arr.			8 33							10 27 10 54										1 56			
Dunbridge	dep.			7 32				9 25						11 6										1 49
Dean	,,			7 37				9 33						11 14										1 57
SALISBURY	arr.		2 17	7 57				9 50	10 3				11 31	11 55										2 14

1906 Timetable

Early photo of Portsmouth Harbour station.

Portsmouth Harbour, with a 'Paddleboat' about to depart.

4

between the LSWR and the LBSC, as they raced to provide the direct service, is tangled and beyond the scope of these pages. But mention should be made of Havant, which produced mayhem on a splendid scale.

But in the end a joint line was arranged. The routes converged at Portcreek Junction, went over a moat and through an earthwork ('the world's smallest tunnel') and then headed due south through open fields. There was a temporary railhead at Copnor (still commemorated by a pub called The Terminus). At Fratton there was a major westward curve to take the line along the route of a moribund canal. At Landport the main section was laid out on the area of the old canal basin. Incidentally, this canal was part of a strategic water route to connect Portsmouth with Chichester – a fascinating story in itself.

A tramway connected Portsmouth town with Clarence Pier and the Isle of Wight ferries. But there was pressure for a direct railhead. The Admiralty was staunch in their insistence that the defences should not be breached. Today we smile at such things, but in a naval town of the period, fear of invasion was very real. But the line was only allowed to proceed by dint of a sharp climb and a run along a rampart until it ended in Portsmouth Harbour station. Two spurs came off this line to serve the internal rail system of Portsmouth Dockyard.

Now this forms the basis of the railway as it exists today. The only major development thereafter was the building of the Fratton and Southsea Railway. This was a particularly interesting line and the traces are still there – you can see the course instantly on a modern road map or aerial photograph. Its closing left one other legacy. Portsmouth Town was renamed Portsmouth and Southsea. The fact that everybody in the area still calls it Town Station, I find almost impressive.

P & S' sea high level circa 1954. M7 30029

Portsmouth & Southsea as seen from High Level, June 1981.
The low level now only has two platforms.

7

The triangle at Fratton provided the basis of the carriage and loco sheds – the latter jointly owned by the two original companies. This state of affairs was rare in Great Britain and, as far as I know, only shared by one other shed in Scotland. There were several minor lines which came off the mainline. As well as the two dockyard spurs, there was an additional short line which ran down from the Harbour Station into HMS Vernon. Portsmouth Gas Works had its own internal system and there was a siding which served the claypits and brickworks immediately to the south of it. Adjacent to the World's Shortest Tunnel was a further MOD establishment at Hilsea and this too was rail served.

Finally, to complete the picture, there were other independent lines. The Clarence Pier Tramway has already been mentioned. Eventually there was a Portsmouth and Horndean Tramway which had great pretensions of being a light railway on its own account. A short stub of railway was said to have existed in the Baffins area, but details are sketchy. There were two miniature railways. The Southsea Miniature Railway ran at Children's Corner. Indeed, it still runs. The other line was the very attractive but ephemeral line which ran at Hilsea Lido.

Portsmouth Corporation ran its own tramway system which was replaced by some much lamented trolley buses.

The island on which most of Portsmouth sits has a finite size. Thus it has been particularly vulnerable to the demands of the motor car. This has wrought more change than the extensive attentions of the Luftwaffe could achieve. The demands of transport on the area have meant that every resource is used to its maximum. So today the trains run at close headway and are well supported. There is a sort of Park and Ride situation at Hilsea, but in reality the whole area is used by suburban services.

From Jacobs Ladder, Nov. 1988

9

Dawn over Portsmouth & Southsea station 11/87.

The pattern of the wider services too has remained unchanged. There is heavy traffic to Waterloo, Southampton and Brighton. Everywhere east of Pompey is electrified, everything west isn't. There have long been plans to electrify the lines to Eastleigh and Southampton.

But this is now. I can stand on the steps of the footbridge at the throat of Portsmouth and Southsea, (known as Jacobs Ladder) and stare at the modern signal box located in a curious dent in the old canal wall. As the Guildhall clock strikes the hour, the box dissolves in front of me. In its place is the little turntable with a Drummond T9 taking water next to it. The coaches are being shunted by a weary M7 and the spotters notebook is grubby in my hands.

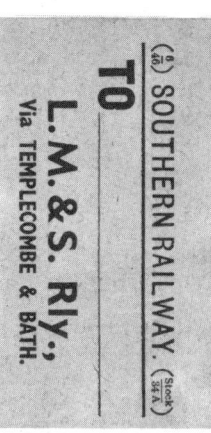

P & S' sea high level from the old platform 5.2.88

12

P & S' sea station sign preserved at Knebworth 6.81

13

Portsmouth & Southsea high level 3.5.52 (Photo Real)

14

Jacob's Ladder 2.88

Just for once, the morning was really warm and sunny. There was barely a breath of wind as the tyres of the trolley bus rumbled over the cobbles of Greetham Street. From the upper deck you could see over a high railway wall and watch a 2-Nol slowing down after its languid journey from Chichester. The bus stopped outside the Sussex pub and there was little traffic in the early 1950s to make crossing the road difficult for pedestrians. Commercial Road dipped sharply under the Harbour Extension line and the flooding at this dip, after heavy rain, provided splendid entertainment.

But our steps were leading to the booking hall of the Town Station. As you went in, the bare boards echoed hollowly. The booking staff were ensconced in an elaborate wooden container that once was impressive but now wasn't. There were several tiny windows available for the taking of money, but inevitably only one was open for business.

Out on the concourse there was the usual gubbins of the Southern Railway, virtually untouched by nationalization. The great swinging boards with the paper timetables stuck on were a model of clarity. Just in case you weren't sure, there were the individual train boards religiously posted in slots. Any of the staff could quote train times. Any, that is, except the two ladies who worked in the information office. They regarded all enquirers as unwanted interruptions to their knitting and were practised in giving incredible replies with utter confidence.

The machine for stamping out words on strips of aluminium was almost used by habit. Inevitably the last letter would get misspelled. Over the parcels department was a temporary roof. This had been put up following bomb damage. It was only supposed to be there 'until next week when the builders come' – it survived into the 1960s.

16

Portsmouth Tram No. 80 decorated and illuminated for
visit of French Fleet. View inside North End Depot

17

T9 on Portsmouth section of train to Plymouth. 12.15 dep Portsmouth & Southsea 24.6.49
(Photo Real)

18

The Town Station was, above all, a place of sounds. The two high level platforms produced frequent deafening rumbles echoing inside the cheerless dark box. It was almost at the threshold of pain at times. Trains going up and down the bank would be heralded by a warning bell situated by the signal box. This made the silences between that much more noticeable. There wasn't the endless roar of traffic noise that exists today and even modest sounds seemed so distinctive. At the North end of Jacob's Ladder was a small engineering works and the perpetual musical screeching of cutting metal could be plainly heard.

The lowly EMU's – the Hals and Bils – would scuttle furtively into the low level platforms with their 'tikatikatika' from the brake resevoir. Steam locomotives seemed to go about their business gently. Even when hauling a heavy train up the bank they would inevitably be coasting to a stop. No, the only noise of note was the occasional lifting safety valve and the M7 flyshunting a couple of wagons across the station throat. On one occasion the engine was derailed under Jacob's Ladder, shutting several platforms entirely. Word soon spread around the local schools and by 4 o'clock, literally hundreds of boys were foregathered on Jacob's Ladder, cheering and countercheering. The breakdown crew, immediately beneath, were offered gratuitous but improbable advice on how to rectify the situation. I seem to recall that the sky became dark with paper aeroplanes being launched at them, before a policeman came and told us to move on. In those days we did....

But such reminiscence was interrupted by the Guildhall clock striking at 9.00 am. The train would be leaving in three minutes time. Walking out onto the platform there came that distinct aroma from the fish market nearby. The sounds went flat on the open platform and there was one of those momentary pauses in the activity of the station. The only thing of interest to be seen

Section of Old Canal Wall, Somers Rd Bridge, 1987

Hants DEMU at Fratton, Nov. 1988

31800 on Fratton Shed c. 1959

A class 33 on the avoiding loop at Fratton. It will be taking a Portsmouth Harbour–Cardiff train in early afternoon. This service is now operated by Sprinter trains.

23

was the 20003 – the electric loco built in 1948. This looked immensely long and black, tucked behind the signal box.

The engine for our train was a T9. The trip would not be exciting but there would be that loud melodious clanking from the coupling rods as they twinkled round their small crank throw. The coaches would inevitably be old LSWR stock with their three-radius roofs. There were but a few concessions for the passing years. The door of the leading compartment would slam behind us with a massively dull 'kerchonk' and for a few moments the silence was satisfying. Somewhere underneath the seats the stem heating pipes would gently crackle to themselves, whilst the dull photographs of exotic, far-away places like Budleigh Salterton and Lulworth Cove provided little relief from the equally dull woodwork and upholstery. If ever compartments suffered from stuffy depression it was these.

But this had little time to impinge on us because the windows would be slid down and thereafter heads would remain outside the windows, despite the official injunction written above. This was virtually the only law that we disobeyed regularly in those more innocent days. But the spectacles are becoming rosy; there were sins of boistrous spirits that made it compulsory for all railway staff to hate the sight of two or more boys together.

The guard's whistle was brief and the departure unceremonious. The short train would ease gently away and that was that. On our left we looked for our favourite spot on Jacob's Ladder. A crowning glory was seeing a couple of friends there and being triumphant at their failure to come with us. Verbal counterplay was brief but fun and we were soon between the high walls. We would be passing such architectural gems as Port Royal Street (one of those evocative names that was totally at odds with its drabness) and Omega Street Junior School. We somehow never

Terrier on Fratton shed 26.12.49 (Photo Real)

25

Early photo of Fratton. This scene remains virtually unchanged (Photo anon)

forgave the Luftwaffe for missing this wretched establishment. It certainly made a mess everywhere else.

Ahead the loco was gently swaying as we ran down under Somers Road Bridge. It was a spot some 100 yards to the south of the line that a first memory was of looking out at nothing but white woolly clouds while this evocative noise of trains echoed around continually, and sowed the seed of a fruit that was to last a lifetime.

But on the north side of the line we were passing Sydenham Terrace. This seemed totally out of place with its ornate ironwork balconies, looking like a transplant from New Orleans and like no other frontage in Portsmouth. Four times a day the massed phalanx of Dockyard workers on bicycles would take full possession of the road for a minute.

But, somewhere up ahead, a bell was warning the barrow crossing at Fratton Station that we were approaching. The train would ease up as it ran under Fratton Bridge and into Platform 1, which sported a private licensed refreshment room – unusual in a station first along the line from the terminus. Across the tracks there was a glimpse of a 12-car EMU dripping from its recent trip through the black washing shed. On several occasions I watched Bulleid light pacifics being cleaned thus. There is some dispute as to whether this was intended as part of the original design.

A late-running Brighton train (a rare thing) pulled up on the adjacent platform and there was the usual scramble of people changing trains to continue their journey westwards. In the distance was the haze of Fratton shed and the outline of the steam crane coaling a King Arthur (seen many times and so held in contempt, of course). Waiting for the road was a pair of Terrier tanks. After we had departed they would scoot up the line at 60 mph, keeping a path in the tight timetable. Even at speed they ran like watches and would spend the day fussing up and down the Hayling branch.

The tracks would all converge again until we were propelled under an impressive signal gantry and run past 'The Rec' – St. Mary's Recreation Ground – another hallowed spot for the enthusiast. This gave way to a cemetery whilst on our right the grim walls of the prison was taken for granted and ignored. Once past Copnor bridge there was a short lull as housebacks ran past. We were looking towards the next landmark and that was the gas works.

This establishment at Hilsea was seved by a compact rail system (as well as an extensive overhead Telfer track). Motive power was in the form of two pretty little Beyer Peacock tanks –'Farlington' and 'Sir John Baker'. Their normal home was a somewhat sunken lean-to, adjacent to the main line. They were kept in sparkling condition and were the only part of the system that was. To watch them blast up the bank, with a sharp curve at the top, propelling six wagons to the Ovens, was to behold some pretty raw forces at work. Accidents were few, apart from the occasional derailment. I used to revel in crawling over them, as a toddler, when they were out of service. Perhaps the high point of recent years had been when a boiler was completely overhauled and retubed by Gas Works fitters, rather than return it to the makers.

But on the day of our journey there was just a brief flash of green behind the coke piles before we swept past Green Lanes Crossing. The signalman here had the unenviable job of operating crossing gates for a constant stream of heavy lorries, against a close headway of a busy train service. As a result, his soul was mightily twisted. It's funny, but there never seemed to be anyone else on duty there. Whilst waiting for the little wicket gate to open to allow pedestrians across, one was always confronted by waves of loathing scowling from the box.

The location acheived a kind of fame when a large unexploded bomb was found in wartime. Being close to the gas holders, it was not a healthy spot to be in. But supplies for the dockyard still

The site of the old Copnor level crossing 2.88

Looking north from Hilsea 2.88

32

The World's Shortest Tunnel 2.88

Newly introduced Sprinter, Cosham, Nov. 1988

34

had to get through. Volunteer Southern Railway crews took goods trains past the spot, whilst lying full length on the footplate.

But none of the above conveys the misery of the spot fully. Gas works made quite a loud noise, but the real drawback was the smell. It was all pervasive and clung in clothes and hair. Right next door to the level crossing were a couple of prefabs and we just couldn't conceive how anyone could stand living there.

For us on the train there would just be a brief moment of that horrible smell and we were past. Up behind the coal piles another little tank engine was dumped. This had worked at MOD Hilsea and is happily still with us. It carries the name Lord Fisher and now resides at the East Somerset Railway.

After passing the gas works on the right, we immediately crossed the compartment to see if there was anything in MOD Hilsea. It didn't produce a loco very often, but the occasional Q1 would reward us by being present. We ignore Hilsea Halt entirely. In the early 'fifties it seemed permanently unused, although it gave a useful little service to works surrounding the airfield.

We took for granted what must have been interesting aerial activity of the period. The de Havilland Rapides would creak about their business of joy rides, trips to the Isle of Wight and further adventures. I had this vague memory of bouncing along inside a creaking fuselage, sitting on a whicker seat. . . . From time to time a private Tiger Moth or Auster would float in and out, but the only time when our attention would be distracted from our beloved railway was when an adapted barrage balloon would be used for parachute training. Alas, there would come a time when a couple of aircraft, returning from a longer journey, would skid across the Eastern Road and give a good excuse to shut the field down.

Looking west from Cosham. Between the two bridges the Horndean Tramway crossed over the line. No trace remains today 2.88

Cosham Station looking east 2.88

37

But our train journey gave little time for thought. Immediately after Hilsea we were slowing down for Portcreek Junction. After the momentary shadow of the World's Smallest Tunnel we were rumbling over the two bridges and swinging slowly to the left. Today we were in luck and being held for Signals at Cosham Junction. There was a train coming along the line from Havant. This could produce all sorts of exotica. I caught my only glimpse of a Bulleid 'Leader' in steam near here. Today it was 30912 'Downside'. Once electrification had come to the Portsmouth to Waterloo line, the Schools class became something of a rarity in Portsmouth –unless you were prepared to be at Fratton Station at 5 o'clock in the morning to watch the paper train come in.

We soon had our road and eased gently along the mild piece of track towards Cosham. We slid under a friendly little overbridge and then into the station. This would often be the end of our journey. It cost 4d to travel from Fratton to Cosham by train or trolleybus and thus it was an easily affordable expedition. Out here in the wilds you would lose the chance of seeing EMUs (no loss whatsoever in our scale of values then) but get the chance to see such South Coast traffic that there was.

But today our ambitions were higher. We moved off briskly over the level crossing and passed the abatments of the bridge which once took the Portsmouth and Horndean Light Railway over the line. There would now be a lull in the proceedings. Wymering racecourse had long since vanished without trace and Portchester was a brief halt.

Our next landmark came when we emerged out onto the two brick viaducts at Fareham. We slowed for the tortuous right curve which lead us, flanges squealing, into Fareham station. On the Gosport line an N Class 2-6-0 was waiting for the road towards Southampton. Over in the

Class 700 30306 at Fareham 15.6.53 (Photo Pamlin)

Class 700 30350 at Fareham 1959, on special

Whistle screaming, a Bulleid pacific thunders through Eastleigh station.

41

A mixed train on the Hayling branch; the Terrier was one of the Fratton regulars.

42

Havant Yard

Havant, 1958. A Terrier normally shedded at Fratton

44

Havant Station, 1874, showing Hayling Branch

45

yard we saw a little B4 0-4-0t idly shunting; an unexpected visitor. On the left the two steam cranes were busy doing nothing but gently blowing off steam. Ahead stretched the various routes and we were looking for our road.

The track going straight in front of us singled out and went through the Pig and Whistle tunnels and on towards Eastleigh. In a year's time I would be caught in the longer tunnel by an ailing Drummond 700 which would leave me gasping for air in a refuge. My reward would be the sight of the 'Daily Western' down from South Wales, being stopped at Knowle Halt for a customer bound for the adjacent mental hospital. A nine coach train stopped at a one coach halt was a most singular occurrence.

Also in front of us was the route which bypassed the tunnel, as well as some oil sidings in a little fenced compund surrounded by earth banks. But we were destined for better things on this journey.

On this particular day the destination was Salisbury; a place for finding the unusual. You could nip into a Bulleid Tavern Car for ten minutes whilst locos were being changed or watered to the accompanying sound of the wheeltapper. It was a convenient place for BR to put oddments. The preserved Adams 4-4-0 languished here as, thirty five years later, did Clan Line.

But those lines heading west out of Fareham could lead to a variety of destinations. Some, like the Romsey to Andover line, had no particular trainspotting merit, but reeked of Southern Railway. The line up to Didcot was uninspiring to youthful eyes – almost an endurance test. Somehow or other I managed to get a train trip of some sort on all the minor lines – Gosport, Meon Valley, Bishops Waltham, Lymington etc. They involved a certain amount of cadging illegal lifts. In the case of the Bishops Waltham branch my journey consisted of an illicit ride on a permanent way trolley.

Perhaps all this should be put into a context of some sort. The lines that flourished westwards out of Portsmouth were very personal territory to us. They never seemed to get much coverage in print, with the exception of Southampton which we mostly ignored. Today, the vast proliferation of railway literature, organized specials and the like have removed some of the mystery of it all. We felt almost isolated. Who else knew that the numbered bridges between Fareham and St Denys had one missing?

Yes, in those younger and more naive days, we were trainspotters. We were no experts in timetabling of the 1930s, or in the types of similar coaches. But there was this affinity with the whole part of the railway. It was sometimes enough to sit on a grassy bank and just take in the warmth and smell of a backwater line. When the rose bay willow-herb grew tall and the bees buzzed over old sleepers, smelling of oil and warm creosote, the communion was complete. If forced we would probably admit that a moving train in the landscape wasn't an absolute necessity.

The picture had been drawn with fine lines and the shading is gentle. But of course, there were so many more snapshots – little icons of affection fondly remembered. There were so many, but included... standing on Eastleigh station as Bullied Pacifics screamed through on the Bournemouth trains, bucketing wildly over the pointwork at the north end... and ten minutes later seeing the City of Truro materialize as if by magic, on a train to Southampton Terminus... of interesting locos stored at Fratton Shed and a couple of glorious weeks when the normal very strict ban on enthusiasts was eased... of a cold day at Fareham when a special train spilled out passengers in period costume... of the Castle Class which somehow got passed east of Salisbury to be impounded at Fratton shed because of being over gauge... of Granges in Great

Western livery on Platform 5 at the town station… of that Bullied Leader… of just so much, now half forgotten but coming back to life as I type these lines.

Perhaps there is something to be learnt here. The great locations will look after themselves. It is the very ordinary nature of the railway that may exist inside our head which can pass into oblivion so easily. Be in no doubt, this is not just the perogative of the steam railway of the '40s and '50s, which becomes so important with the passing years. Exactly the same thing applies today. It often takes a deliberate effort to record the local station today. Somehow the years slip by and the changes occur imperceptibly.

The pace of change more or less continued unaltered. Yes, the ordinary working steam locomotive is gone, but that was only part of the picture. The fascination of those thin steel ribbons remains to claim our attention as much as it ever did.

Postscript: As this text was being prepared, Portsmouth and Southsea station was undergoing a substantial rebuild, and electrification of the Portsmouth – Southampton and Eastleigh lines was authorized. The story continues.

Southampton Central with schools class 'Downside' c. 1960

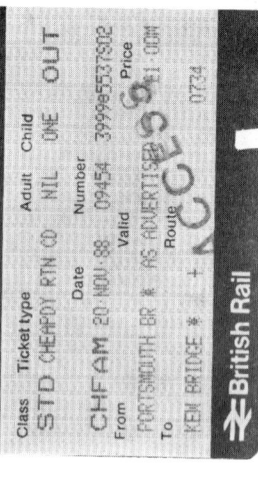

Modern Computerised Tickets

50

Victoria-Portsmouth Train, 1951

51

SOUTHERN RAILWAY.
(3/24)
Stock 787
TO
CHELTENHAM
Via ANDOVER JUNCTION.
SOUTHERN RAILWAY.
(8/27)
Stock 787
TO
CREWE
Via
SOUTHERN RAILWAY.
(8/25)
Stock 787
TO
EASTLEIGH
SOUTHERN RAILWAY.
(9/43)
Stock 787
TO
BOURNEMOUTH WEST
SOUTHERN RAILWAY.
(8/25)
Stock 787
TO
BRISTOL
(STAPLETON ROAD, Via SALISBURY)
SOUTHERN RAILWAY.
(2/45)
Stock 787
TO
BRIGHTON

Table 54   **Week Days**

Table 54— continued	PORTSMOUTH, FAREHAM, SOUTHAMPTON, EASTLEIGH, ANDOVER, SALISBURY, WESTBURY, TROWBRIDGE and BATH SPA

Week Days – continued

Station	Times (am unless shown)
28 Brighton .. .. dep	5 10 5 10 5 10 10 … 5 50 … 6d17 6 17 6 17 … 7d 4 7 7 7 7d7 47 … 7 47
28 Worthing Central	5 33 5 33 5 33 … 6d48 6 34 6 34 6 34 … 7d26 7 26 7 7d7 26 … 8 6
28 Barnham	5 58 5 58 5 58 … 6d48 6 58 7d20 7d20 … 7d50 7 50 7 7d50 8 29 … 8d48
28 Chichester	6 7 6 7 6 7 … 6d57 7d 8 7 8 7d29 7d29 … 8d 28 8 2 86 8d38 … 8d50
Portsmouth Harbour .. dep	6 53 7 37 8 … 7 30 *(from Southampton Terminus)* … 7 56 8 38 8 … 8 38 8 53 9 39 15 … 9 30
Portsmouth & Southsea	6 56 7 57 11 … 7 33 … 7 45 7 58 6 8 11 … 8 41 8 56 9 9 19 18 … 9 33
Fratton	… … … … … … … … … … … … … … …
Hilsea Halt	7 4 7 13 7 18 … 7 42 … 7 57 8 6 8 14 8 18 … 8 48 9 4 9 14 9 25 … 9 42
Cosham	7 8 … … … 7 48 … 7 57 8 10 … 8 23 … 8 53 9 8 … 9 30 … …
Portchester	7 14 7 21 7 27 … 7 55 8 3 3 8 16 8 228 29 … 8 59 9 14 6 9 39 36 … 9 52
Fareham .. .. {arr	7 16 7 21 7 27 … 7 56 8 3 8 13 8 21 8 29 … … … … … …
Fareham	… … … … … … … … … … … … … … …
Knowle Halt	… … … … … … … … … … 9 24 … 9 44 … …
Botley	7 24 … … … … … … … … 9 32 … 9 52 … …
Eastleigh .. .. arr	7 32 … … … 8 17 8 31 … 8 33 … … … … … …
Swanwick .. .. dep	… 7 33 … … … … … … 8 36 … 9 6 … … … …
Bursledon	… 7 37 … … 8 13 … … … 8 39 … 9 9 … … … …
Hamble Halt	… 7 40 … … 8 16 … … … 8 43 … 9 13 … … … …
Netley	7 32 7 43 … … 8 19 … … 8 348 45 … 9 15 … 9 34 … 10 5
Sholing	… 7 46 … … 8 23 … … … 8 49 … 9 19 … … … …
Woolston	7 37 7 49 … … 8 25 … … 8 398 51 … 9 21 … 9 39 … 1011
Bitterne	… 7 52 … … 8 28 … … … 8 55 … 9 25 … … … …
St. Denys	7 42 7 55 … … 8 31 … … 8 448 59 … 9 27 … 9 44 … 1017
Northam .. .. dep	… 7 57 … … … … … … … … … … … … …
Southampton Central {arr	… 8 0 … … … … … … … … … … … … …
Terminus {dep	… … … … … … … … … … … … … … …
Southampton Central .. arr	7 47 … … … 8 36 … 8 498 4 … 9 33 … 9 49 … 1023
32 Bournemouth Central .. arr	8 53 … … … 10 5 … 10 5 … … 10A30 … 10A30 … 1114
Southampton Central .. dep	7 50 … … … 8 39 … 8 50 … … 9 33 … 10 0 … 1025
Millbrook	… … … … 8 41 … … … … 9 36 … … … …
Redbridge	… … … … 8 45 … … … … 9 39 … … … …
Eastleigh .. .. dep	7 40 … … 8 34 … 8 41 … … … 9 40 … … … 1041
Chandlers Ford	7 45 … … … … … … … … 9 47 9 52 10 11 …
Romsey	7 528 2 … 8 44 … 9 2 … … 9 5210 11 … 1041
Mottisfont	7 59 … … 8 52 … … … … … … … … …
Horsebridge	8 4 … … 8 59 … … … … 10 4 … … …
Stockbridge	8 10 … … 9 10 … … … … 10 9 … … …
Fullerton	8 17 … … 9 17 … … … … 10 11 … … …
Clatford	8 24 … … 9 24 … … … … 10 19 … … …
Andover Town	8 29 … … 9 29 … … … … 10 23 … … …
Andover Junction .. arr	8 32 … … 9 32 … … … … 10 27 … … …
Dunbridge	8 8 … … … … 9 14 … … 10 9 … …
Dean	8 13 … … … … 9 19 … … 10 23 … 11 5
Salisbury .. .. arr	8 27 … … … … 9 27 … … 10 36 … 11 5
35 Exeter Central .. arr	… … … … … … … 1 8 …
35 Ilfracombe	… … … … … … … … …
35 Plymouth	… … … … … … … 3 15 …
32, 34 Bournemouth Central .. dep	… … … … 7 43 … … 9852 … 1115
Salisbury {arr	… … … 10 10 1037 … … 1145
{dep	… … … 10 10 1039 … … 1157
Warminster {arr	… 9 42 … 1041 1050 … … 12 0
Dilton Marsh Halt	… 9 55 … 10 58 … … 12 6
Westbury {arr	… 9 55 … 11 5 … … 1213
{dep	… 10 3 … 11 5 … … 1217
Trowbridge {arr	… 10 10 … 1115 … … 1225
{dep	… 10 10 … 1115 … … …
Bradford-on-Avon	… 10 16 … 1122 … … …
Avoncliff Halt	… 10 19 … 1125 … … …
Freshford	… … … … … … …
Limpley Stoke Halt	… … … … … … …
Bathampton	… … … … … … …
Bath Spa .. .. arr	… 10 33 … 1139 … … 1241
Bristol (Temple Meads) ..	… 10 52 … 1158 … … 1 6
Bristol (Stapleton Road) ..	… … … … … … …
Newport	… 12 23 … 1C57 … … 1 57
Cardiff (General)	… 12 44 … 2C18 … … 2 18

A Applies Mondays to Fridays until 26th April, 1963. Weekdays commencing 29th April, 1963
C On Saturdays arr Newport 1 36 pm and Cardiff (General) 1 55 pm
d Change at Fratton
F Via Fordingbridge
G Change at Barnham and Fratton
K On Mondays to Fridays dep Barnham 8 21 am, Chichester 8 29 am. Change at Fratton
H Change at Southampton Central
S Saturdays only

(Through Train Weymouth (dep 8 15 am) to Bristol (Temple Meads) (Table 33))
(To Reading General)
(Through Train Salisbury to Bristol (Temple Meads))
(Miniature Buffet Car Train Portsmouth and Southsea to Cardiff (General))

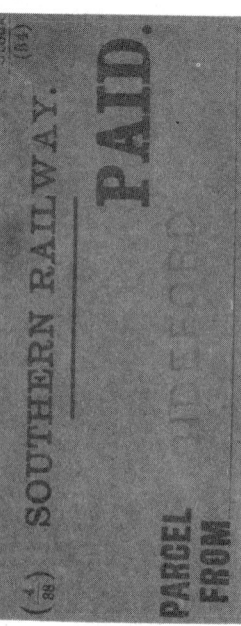

54

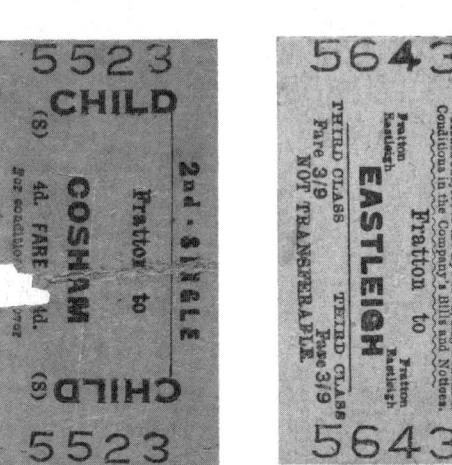

Portsmouth & Southsea High Level, looking East. This photo was taken in February 1988, just before the rebuild affected it.

London Brighton & South Coast Railway.

Brighton to

Bristol

(G. W. R. via Kensington.)

London Brighton and South Coast Railway.

East Grinstead to

Portsmouth Har.

London Brighton & South Coast Railway.

East Grinstead to

Crowborough

London Brighton & South Coast Railway.

East Grinstead to

Streatham Common

Southern Railway Luggage Label

58

SOUTHERN RAILWAY.

(3/40)

PORTSMOUTH & SOUTHSEA

TO

Stock 787

London Brighton & South Coast Railway.

East Grinstead to

Crawley